Contents

Joan Sikand's
SUNFLOWER
A Memoir

Published by
Path Press, Inc.

First Published 2020.

Library of Congress Cataloging-in-Publication Data

Names: Sikand, Joan, author.
Paik, Joyce C., 1929- illustrator.

Title: Sunflower, a memoir / Joan P. Sikand, Joyce C. Paik.

Description: Evanston, Illinois : Path Press, Inc., 2020. | Summary:
"The book is the story of the author's mother who was born in Korea
and was able to immigrate to the United States based upon her skill as
an artist. She married a Korean migrant who was a Christian minister
and raised four girls. The author includes paintings by the mother and
poetry composed by the author"-- Provided by publisher.

Identifiers: LCCN 2020011527 | ISBN 9780910671217 (paperback)
Subjects: LCSH: Paik, Joyce C., 1929-

1. Korean Americans--Biography. 2. Korean American
women--Biography. 3. Spouses of clergy--United States--Biography.

Classification: LCC E184.K6 S55 2020 | DDC 305.8957/0730092
[B]--dc23 LC record available at https://lccn.loc.gov/2020011527

Dedication

*To My Mother
Immortal -
Eternally Wise*

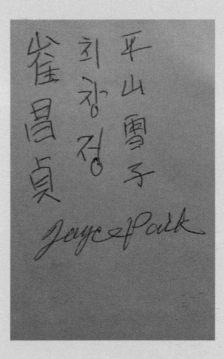

Introduction

In every age since before the time of Moses, God has sent a revelation. The world is eternal, without end nor beginning. Humanity is only here for a time, subject to constant change. The chaos of our age is that we are lost in a craze of super-ego. Anger, perverse attachment, and base negativity control our lives. The result is spasmotic dysfunction. Modern society is chronically ill. Medicine is the road to riches. The prisons are very full. The youth are disoriented, mutilated and abandoned. Confusion is everywhere. Our planet, Mother Earth, is degraded beyond belief. Culture, music and art, are all but dead; no more song, no more pleasure, joy, wonder. The human soul is forgotten. Sexuality has gone amok. The consequence is ceaseless pain and suffering. And, of course, nothing is new. Man's folly has always occurred. The results change, and now humanity is well on the cusp of extinction.

Look up and see the sky; sun, moon, stars, clouds. All the planets and constellations surround us. The elements, in their principal; earth, air, water, fire, manifest and incarnate. Mind is energy and force. Heaven and earth are inter-connected;

we are all one. Through time, religions remind humanity of
the greater power of God, which is within all and each of
us; Christianity, Judaism, Islam, etc. Their prophets inspire
a deeper reflection to existence. There was a rebel Dutch
master, Vincent Van Gogh who witnessed universality in the
sunflower. Having grown up in the church, Van Gogh was
made aware of the existence of God, but how to experience
God? In some aspect, as the simple, yellow sunflower.

Love is the answer to renewal. To release annihilating ego,
forgiveness and humility must occur. Mother is the beginning
of love. As an artist, my mother created canvases in oil, and
wonderful pastels. Her story is remarkable. Born Chwe Chang
Jung, my mother says that she made up her birthday, January
17, 1929, in order to apply for her visa to enter and emigrate
to the US. At that time, in Shinuiju, now North Korea, there
were few hospitals and little record keeping of birth certificates.
She was born at home, in a thatch hut, her mother going into
labor on a mattress on the floor with a twisted sheet hung over
the ceiling beam to hang onto, and a stick between her teeth to
bear the pain. Once, at seven years, she followed her mother by
train to Pyongyang. An old lady admired my mother's hands.
She told her fortune; she would lead a long and unusual life.
Born of her father's second marriage to a younger woman, my
mother hardly knew her father, who died by the time she was
17. Japan had by that time fully annexed Korea. In this occupied
police state, my mother was sent as a beautiful teenager to the
farmlands to escape Japanese sex work. There she learned to
plant sesame, cucumbers, radishes, sunflowers. Her elder brother
was sent to Manchuria during Japanese occupation to avoid
conscription. When WWII ended he did not return to Shinuiju,
but went to Seoul and sent for his family to meet him there.

For my mother, the flight to Seoul was terrifying. My
grandmother, mother and her younger brother left their home
and started south by train, but when they reached the 38th

Parallel, my mother was lost and separated. The communist soldiers caught her and threw her into prison. Conditions were filthy, with poor food, and so crowded, she couldn't sit in the prison cell; you were forced to stand. She was released after several months. She could not locate her mother. Without protection, she was again caught by the communists and again put in prison. A communist soldier told her if she had sex with him he would release her. She refused. After several weeks, she was released. This time, her mother had arranged for an advisor to receive her. At night, the advisor led her to a river where they would cross to pass into south Korea. They needed to start their walk across the river at high tide, the water rising above her head, the advisor holding her hand and leading. She did cross. Her feet were torn through the grass sandals. After selling her one possession, a box of face powder, she managed to get to Seoul, and was reunited with her mother and brothers. There were six now, in one tiny cramped and dirty room. During the bombing, my mother was forced to stay underground, and starved; there was no food. When the sirens stopped and she climbed out, Seoul was a field of corpses; bodies and body parts strewn everywhere, as far as eyes could see. After the bombing, all the buildings, made of thatch and wood, the palaces, shrines, temples, the villages centered around a water mill downstream from a mountain river, were flattened. Only the church remained standing. Miracle. When the fighting stopped, Korea was in total ashes.

As Korea started to rebuild, my mother entered and won a national art contest. She could do portraits, and the American soldiers were glad for the pictures. At that time, the only place with electric lights was the local police station, and she would go there to work at her art. She received an art scholarship to the US, and finally left Korea. At Radford Women's College in Virginia, she found studies confusing and difficult, and she contacted the only person she knew in the US, my father, who was then studying at McCormick Theological Seminary in Evanston, Ill, towards his Master of Arts. They had met at Taegu where he had served as chaplain and translator for the US Air Force. She went to Chicago hoping to get a job. Instead, my father asked my mother to marry him. So, my mother borrowed a white wedding gown and a set of pearls from a church member, and married. Afterwards, everyone ate dumpling soup and kimchi in the church basement. At the studio to take their wedding photo, my father stood on a box to appear taller. They were both virgins.

His diploma read;

> *'This diploma is awarded in the confidence that you will so use this right to teach that you may show yourself "approved unto God, a work, man that needeth not to be ashamed, handling aright the word of truth." We follow you with our affectionate interest and our fervent prayers that the grace of the Lord Jesus Christ may rest abundantly upon your ministry.'*

My parents moved to Fort Worth, Texas, where my mother hoped to continue her studies at Texas Christian University. Her immediate pregnancies to my older sisters, Mary, Esther and Martha, prevented her from continuing. In violation of her student visa, she was subject to deportation. However, the church contacted Texas Congressman, Jim Wright. On hearing their story, he sponsored a bill which stayed their deportation, and allowed them to apply for citizenship. My mother sat the US immigration exam three times before she passed. They returned to Chicago to help my uncle and his young family.

My father received an offer of employment from the American Bible Society, and they were off to New York City. Starting in a small one bedroom in Brooklyn for $50/month, my sister Mary is born, and then myself in 1963. We are six in a tiny one bedroom. Much to the shock of my parents, we were four sisters. My mother's last pregnancy with me caused her huge pain and bleeding, ending in a C-section. The doctor advised my parents they would not have a son. Largely ignored, Esther took care of me, changing my diapers, and carrying me around. As an infant, I adored her. My father bought a house on mortgage in Flushing. It was a three bedroom, attached, corner house. It had a front and back yard. The basement was cool during the hot summers. My mother was very happy. As a little girl, I would collect dandelion bouquets for her. The front yard had a pine tree.

My mother continued her art in Greenwich Village, doing portraits on the street. My father came to her one day; her mother in Korea had died. She finished the portrait crying. There were quite a number of Jewish hotels in the Catskills, country clubs where rich Jewish people went to have a vacation with their families. Gottlieb, Lowenthal, Schwartz, Rosenstein. The Fallsview Hotel was still open for a resident artist. The Fallsview had tennis courts, indoor and outdoor pools, indoor skating rink, a lake with paddle boats, several buildings, surrounded by the Catskills. She set up her easel in the Main Lobby, and waited for guests to ask for portraits. She continued to sell her paintings. Her paintings were influenced by the high art of later Europe; Degas, Monet, Manet, Mary Cassatt, Picasso. Her landscapes were reminiscent of her youth in Korea. For over 45 years, she trailed from Flushing to Ellenville, 195 to Route 17, every weekend and more. When she started, she took a Greyhound bus, and then later drove our second hand car, which always broke down. Somehow, her paintings and portraits sold, every penny being used to pay off the mortgage and pay the constant bills. During the summers, my mother would sneak my sister Mary and I into the hotel to stay with her. It was so boring, we hated it. We were forbidden to speak to any of the guests. At night, we were allowed to dress up and go to the Main Building, but not to the Lobby. We could get as far as the jewelry shop. Mary and I would stare into the glass casings. There were two enameled poodle pins with diamond eyes; one black, one white. We would take turns arguing which one was better. I really liked the black one better. My mother would bring us cold leftovers from the kitchen, cheese blintzes, gefilte fish, matzos, cocktail hotdogs, stale bagels, smashed cake. We really hated going. Everything in our house was left over from the Fallsview; food, spoons, forks, knives, glasses, linens, towels, blankets. The only remotely fresh item in our house was kimchi; my thumbs would burn and smell from peeling garlic. My father ate kimchi with everything, even Cheerios (the Cheerios came from the Fallsview).

Mary and I shared a bedroom. We slept on old couches which my father found on the street. The room barely held the two couches side by side. Mary would threaten me by pushing the beds apart. I had the habit of rolling over to her bed. By morning she would be flat against the wall like a spider, her bed soaking from my wet dream. One night, I am seven years, Mary and I are in our room. She is drawing at her desk. I am reading Cinderella, her blond hair bundled on top of her head, blue ball gown, white gloves, glass slippers. I hear loud noises downstairs, and I realize that my parents are fighting. My father is smashing my mother with his belt. She is on the floor trying to back away, but there is nowhere to go. She is backed up against the bathroom door. My father's rage is raining blows upon her. I asked my mother, after my father's death, why she never left Daddy. "I had four kids, I'm not so foolish. He had hot temper," is her reply.

Throughout the decades, my mother accepted my father's blows. On Friday, my mother would wait until I came home from school, and then she would leave for the long drive to the Fallsview. She would come back on Sunday morning in time for church, and they would start fighting the minute she entered the door. On Sunday mornings, my father would play Oral Roberts singers on the record player to get us ready. My mother being a portrait artist, was talented at pasting her cuts and bruises. The result was always the same; beautiful samonim, pastor's wife, Mommy. She wore lovely clothes, in wonderful fabrics and patterns. She was good at sewing, and stitched her own jackets and skirts, trimmed with lace, or sequins. She adorned herself with jewelry; earrings, necklace, a broach, at first costume and then later real gold bartered for a painting. There was no issue of forgiveness. She was a part of him, without limit.

All the satanic frustrations of the age; emasculation of man, urgent feminization, moral decay, family collapse, youth alienation and disenfranchisement, perversive fornication, the collapse of the church and Christianity, loss of male authority, unending waste and garbage, constant retail, inflation, job insecurity, sickness, obesity, rampant stupidity, the end of his family line, biting and back-breaking financial strain, were hers with him. He was her husband; she was his wife. And, the people swelled to hear him speak at the pulpit. He could roar loudly God's salvation and promise. All who heard, did believe; they were nourished spiritually. Especially his wife. He was in complete control. She understood him completely. It didn't matter. She would heal. This was not derangement. His anger would soften if you were absolutely obedient to him. There was no question about church; everyone is ready at 8:45 am. I'm wearing a navy blue and red striped dress, with white ankle socks turned down with a lace trim, and black patent leather shoes with a strap across. I loved Sunday School, singing and reading the Bible. During the story of Noah's Ark, I beg Mrs. Henderson to put the animals on the felt board; giraffe, lion, zebra, rhinoceros.

For both my parents, their focus was at all times our family; they loved each of their four daughters, without limit. As parents, they were great. My father never stopped supporting our upbringing and education, paying for our music lessons, which we were terrible at. Oboe, trumpet, flute, piano, tuba.

He attended all the PTA meetings. He came to every play and assembly. He was always there. I would get into the car with my mother and we would collect my father every day at 5:30pm from the subway station. Every night, we had dinner together, the six of us, around the kitchen table. We had strict rules about watching television. Martha could watch TV for hours, eating, chips, soda, candy, and getting fatter and fatter. Sometimes all four of us would watch together; I Love Lucy, The Honeymooners, F Troop, Star Trek. Normally, I hated watching TV; it gave me a terrible headache right away. I'm in the library taking out books, Curious George, Dr. Seuss, Goodnight Moon, The City Mouse and the Country Mouse, The Tortoise and the Hare, Aesop's Fables.

As I was the last born, my mother tried her best to nurse me as long as possible. We loved it. She and I would lie in bed together and fondle and touch for hours, my head between her breasts. I could hear her heart beat, feel her breath. Esther and Martha from their birth were handicapped; they couldn't walk or move normally. They suffered from a congenital neurological disorder. For their entire lives, from the time of their births, they were in constant pain. My mother was always dragging them from hospital to hospital, desperately trying to improve their disabled condition. The medical bills were exhausting. Esther and Martha kept falling everywhere, in school, on the streets, down the stairs. Whenever we sat at the table, they rocked back and forth. I can't stop reading. Reading; All of A Kind Family, Little House, Grimms, Hans Christian Anderson, Greek myths, Pippy Longstocking, Nancy Drew, Little Women, A Tree Grows in Brooklyn, Peanuts, Archie, Brenda Starr, Dick Tracey, Doonesbury, Ibsen, Dostoyevsky, Chekov, Kafka, Longfellow, Walt Whitman, Emily Dickenson, Robert Frost, Langston Hughes, Arthur Miller, Eugene O'Neill, Guy de Maupassat, Flaubert, I. B. Singer, Allen Ginsberg, Jack Karouac.

I am an adolescent and a teenager during America's last great decade, the 1970's. I'm pretty suicidal. I hate myself, and I can't stop thinking about death. I want out. My main interest is Esther's pornographic material. Reading Hustler, Larry Flynt, R. Crumb, Loves Tender Fury. Martha tries her best to kill herself. Esther gets pregnant. Mary hides under the bed. I receive an offer and scholarship to Brandeis, and I'm off. Miracle. Hoffman, Allen, Pollack, Ratner, Bernstein, Jonathan Keith. By 1980 I high-jump into a world of academic elitism, the privilege of a wealthy New England liberal arts college. However, Jewish philanthropy had limits; I was the girl a Jewish mother had to look out for. I apply for and am awarded a fellowship to study in the United Kingdom. In London, at 19, I meet a man from Kenya and fall in love; we truly love each other. Eventually, we marry and become East African wildlife conservationists. We continue on a journey both physical and spiritual. We read; Mahabharat, Bhagavad Gita, Vedas, The Diamond Sutra, The Holy Dalai Lama, The Dhamapada, Confucius, The Heart Sutra, The Kama Sutra, The Quran, Hafiz, Rumi, Kahlil Gibran, The Guru Granth Sahib, Ba'ha'hulla, The I Ching.

We have come to understand together that God is everywhere, at all times, in everyone. The cosmos and the earth are constantly changing. Materiality and causation create ignorance, anger and jealousy; suffering. Religions offer opportunities for prayer, concentration, worship, peace, which are aids to understanding God. Freedom is from understanding impermanence and detachment. Good deeds, actions and choices born of forgiveness, generosity, humility, compassion and love bring enormous and cost-saving benefits; good health, good looks, contentment. Attachment to ego brings misery. Misery causes breakdown, pain and suffering. Joy and contentment are within your power at all times.

The Fallsview closed, after Hurricane Sandy our pine tree was cut down, and The American Bible Society was demolished on Broadway, making way for condominiums. Martha died first in 2008, and then Esther ten years later. Except for the time in Greenwich Village, I have never known my mother to cry. The memories have never overwhelmed her; her stunning longevity. From any distance, I wait to hear her next breath.

The decades have flown by that I have been a wife and mother. I love and am loved, effortlessly. I am always home. I can look at my grown children and say, "I am your Mother. I raised you very well. You need never fear.' I kiss and hold my husband and say, 'Yes, I am your wife. I will never betray you. I will never leave you.' Our days and lives have been filled with joy; their teething and toilets, getting ready for school and work, filling our house, mealtimes (delicious, unpolluted fruits and vegetables from Tigoni, mangoes, seven varieties of citrus, sukuma wiki, pishori rice from Mwea), travelling, finding God, passing through life and death aware and alive. We are so happy. (Miracle!)

My dear reader, welcome! With my Mother's paintings herein; welcome to my song.

YOUR POET
2019

SUNFLOWER

Self Portrait in Blue Evening Gown

1

Verse 1

Intermittance of my dreams,
We awake.
We are alive.
Miracle.

The best you can do is maintain a whisper.
A silent, quiet, suppressed gasp for air.
Trying very, very hard to breathe.
What are my goals?
Parameters? Beginning? End?
Where to continue?
Where? Why? How?
If I went to law school,
He would marry me, and then,
I could be the mother of my dreams –
My family number one and only
Priority of my entire life.
To make love to my husband.
A wife.
A mother.
To care for my children.
To prepare delicious food.

Statue

The dream state is always there, ready, waiting.
We can awake or not.
That is our choice.
No need to tamper with time.

No need to worry.
The irrelevance of success.
My pause, character, experience.
Rooted in myself,
I believe, consider, tarry, wait.
Fixed on God, church, prayer.
Rest.
'Our Father, who art in Heaven,
Thy will be done. Amen!'

Her eyes were in a continuous downcast posture.
To concentrate, meditate. Pray.
To listen to God's voice ringing.
To know.
Hearing sorrow and pain;

Cubism 1955

Grief at utter error and mistake.
Destruction by my very own ambition.
The causation is only mine.
Nowhere to hide.
Nowhere to turn.
I am impatient for your love.
It is mine.

Focus on your nose.
Focus on the tip of your nose.
Aim with the sacred center of your forehead.
Completely aware.
Eyes only to concentrate.
To bring liberation and release.
To know we are indeed –

Free.

Poetry the skill of thought and pen.
The calibration of mind perfected.
Yogic trance.
God's Great and Holy Light.
Inner eye.
Magic.
Wonder.
Absolute.
Someone has to be a poet.
Someone has to listen.
Voices all around.

Not to expect America as some
 Magical kingdom.
The ideal lies simply within yourself,
 Without restriction, restraint, guilt.
Simply you –
To be perfect, kind, gentle, forgiving,
 Pleasant, nice, caring, strong, intelligent,
 Brave.
The cause is your own.
No more; nor less.

The mother's perspective is
So petty and small, mean, jealous,
Clinging.

Esther

Mother and Child

From the streets and garbage
Can rise a monument, a standard.

No structural adhesion.
No way home.

Lost without a clue.
What went wrong?

What? Where? How? Why?
If only it were –

Right, good, blessed, ok.
The foul way is wrong and incorrect.

The person of my identity.
Why? When? Where? How?

It was her humble beauty that caught your breath.
She was lovely.
Her inner I attuned.
She loved cooking.
She knew 1,000 dishes.
Salads, soups, breads, cakes, stews, roasts.
On and on she could cook.
Dozens of grains, pulses, pastas, noodles, roots.
She prayed and prayed for higher physical man.
A golden age.
An age of righteousness, greatness, goodness,
To return.

'Didn't you want to divorce Daddy?'
'I had four kids. I'm not so foolish.
Daddy had hot temper.'

The convulsions of this age.
A tearing down of character.

Perfect rage.

The naivete of my thought and action.
Acceptance of my consequences.
A portrait of Robert.
The loss of my virginity.
Waking up to reality.
Yes; indeed, I finally become my own.

A diamond of one trillion facets.
Brilliant. Stunning. Me.
God in me.

I truly wait for you.
Ignoring fantasies, I am.
Yours.

Eternally and forever.
The verses can come unabated.
Past, future, present.
All are one; and the same.
All are equal, in merit and strength.
All time is just, positive – pure.

1966

1966

Thought. Eternity. Poetry.
Even a father. A son. A daughter.
Great blessings.
Great fortune.

Measuring my time with joy and happiness.
Yes.
I am alive.

Beautiful. Radiant. Sure.
The pain of being born.
The bitterness and joy of
God's holy grace.
Acceptance of god's will.
Whatever the cost. Whatever the price.
Even lots and lots of pain.

And yet, I am not alone.
You are here with me.
Paying the bills.
Having a great time.
Truly in love.
Truly your wife.
I have no thought of leaving.
I do not count the time.
Who knows where the time goes?
Memory a game.
A CURE.

Verse 2

An uncontrollable cry of emotion.
A sharp gasp of air.
Pain.
Relief.
Impending grief.
Eyes of tears, sorrow, guilt, shame.
Lost in a maze of desires.
Consumed by lashings of ego and pride.
Fraud and utter lies.
Falsehoods flooding furiously,
Over my head,
Drowning.
A cosmic ray upon my brow.
Raining bliss.
Driving man to oblivion, despair.
Depression, shrunken, lost, confused.

Sewing

SUNFLOWER

THE ART OF
THE NUDE
Deirdre Robson

Nude [누드]I

18

Inert. Impotent.
Running wild, in hatred and lust.
Mad of sin, fornication, greed,
Stupidity, selfishness, self-righteousness;
Hypocrisy.
Say right of wrong; and, so
Wrong of right.

Contemplating my death, again.
And again.
And yet, again.
Laughter and joy unbecoming.
I am free.
Come with me on this marvelous
Lesson of forgiveness, charm and grace.
The tight, suffocating grip of fantasy and illusion.
Deceiving me. Confusing me. Abusing me.
Screwing me. Frying me.
Eyes rolling upward.
Tongue drooling.
Mad and insane.
Gray hair gone wild.
Talons, horns, claws, tails.
The minotaur ravaging his lovely,
  young Teresa.
Her cries, sighs; her tears.

Rise above the negativity.
Pull ahead of gravity.
Self-control.
Awakening.
Clarity of mind.
Healing.
A lifting of clouds.
Only eyes can see the sun.
Open, aware, awake, alive.
Overcome with relief and healing.
I am free.

Physical exhaustion.
Discarding ego.
Descending. Falling. Releasing.
Re-absorbing. Returning.
Mother Earth re-assuming me.
Embracing me.
Where there is death; and,
Therefore life; so, hope.
And also, miracle.
Love. God. In me and you.
Always, eternal.
So, no fear, least of all.
No fear of death.

SUNFLOWER

Nude [누드]II

21

Living life freely.
So, no fear of death.
To equate life with death,
And so death with life.
No inequalities, hostilities, doubt.
Clearly all is equal, good.
Mystical, intelligence.
Syncretic thoughts.
Cosmic, astral thinking.
Art. Beauty. Love.
My twisted face.
My crooked ways.
Androgenous days.
Neither here nor there.
Neither he nor she.

Evening

Poetry –
The skill of thought and pen.
Scripture becoming myself.
Yes. I am the poet, the lover.
You and me together.
Eternally.

Sunlight filtering through the trees,
Shrubs, plants.
Pleasing. Pure. Fresh. Nice.

Reading

A desperate hope to hold back time.
Stop the march.
Stay in control; expectation; security.
The world had become so dangerous.
Uncertain. Random. Toxic. Violent.
Weird. Lost.
To avoid being thrown into the vast, unknown.
Chaos of suffering.
Creating our miseries.
Locked in disbelief.
Lost beyond belief.
The pain occurring, and occurring, and occurring;
Endlessly.
A hot, overheated age.
Surging humanity.
Craving; growing; multiplying.
Blind.

(I realize, comfortably, that my children will always love me.)

Seasons Spring

Buying yourself a friend.
How much will it cost?
What will be the mark of my religion?
The sign of the times?
Truth or deadly costly lies.
Knowing what you want, diplomatically,
    politically, legally.

SUNFLOWER

Seasons Yellow

Park

She had never lived in such a currency.
Yes. Anything is surely possible.
But, how?
Fear. Fear blurring our lives.
Fear aggravating speech.
Fear creating hatred.
Want. Loss. Dread.
A sudden, sharp gasp for air.
Lungs badly constricted.
Throat dry, sore, tight.
Suffocating. Breath gone.
I suffer.

Paying endlessly for stupid and idiotic mistakes.
Always running for help.
Pointing your finger.
Continuing in an endless gluttony of guilt,
    shame, disgust.
Amoral acts, again, and again.
Disturbing my dreams, I cannot sleep.
No rest.
Only turmoil and loneliness.
Complete zombies.
Numb. Deluded. Dazed. Hopeless. Gone.

Humanity is capable of a higher thought, I am told.
Curiosity. Intelligence. Forgiveness. Creativity. Art.
A painting of herself.
Dreaming of myself.
Lost in delusion of who and what I should be.
Descending into anarchy and chaos.
Relying upon my own.
Thinking and behaving conscientiously.
Confident of right actions.
Good and bad.
Light and dark.
Evil and ego.
Longing and desperate.
I want to feel something.
Who are you?
Then, myself?
Isolation.
Somehow content.
Why should anyone agree?

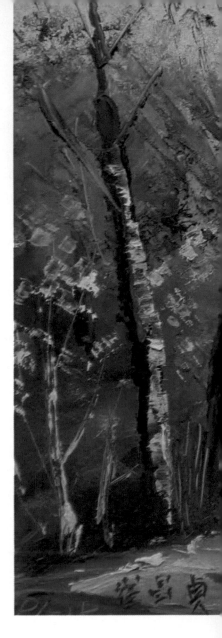

How shall I see you?
Statistically?
Physically?
Mentally?
Spiritually?
Professionally? Humanly?
Emotionally? Psychologically?
Sexually? Lovingly?
Richly rewarded by time and gravity.

Seasons Blue

O. She was lovely.
A heart and mind so pure.
Easy, natural elegance and grace.
Intelligent. Wise. Honest. Happy.
Caring.

It festers upon itself.
It feasts upon itself.
Self-annihilation.
Rotten to the core.
Angry and lost.
Violence and hatred.

Paik   *Flowers*

Do you care? Even, enough?
A barometer of change.
All the rules gone awry.
Complete upheaval.
Revelation.
(That's a very nice little boy. What's his name?)
Serendipity.
Strange concurring times.
Tracked by a trillion stars.

Truly I am not here for life, but for death.

Which attitudes?
Which face?
Self-importance?
Ego? Pride? Ignorance?
Disdain? Envy? Denial?
Humanity without feeling.
Existing without soul.
Time without meaning.

No character; no
spirit, in life.
A numb and
muted time.
An orderly town:
Restaurant, stores,
cars, houses, neat
and tidy schools.
A theatre or two.
Pretense.
Longing to return.
Awake.
Who am I?
What am I?
Where do I belong?
The woman is
gigantically fat.
Her breasts are
very, very large.
Eyes dim, she
has no clue.

Man is bald. Stress.
Worry. Impotence.
Failed erection.
Small, clammy hands.
She does not love you.
Hatred. Loathing.
Disgust.
A crack in the wall may
let the sunshine through.
Yet, we build our
own coffin.
Yet, we suffocate and
blind ourselves.
Neurosis.
Should I feel lonely?
Yet, I am not.
Yet, I'm full.
Yet, okay.

Denial of true causation.
Eating disorders.
Eating and eating.
Consuming always.
How do we know who we are?

Tribal dance.
What is in a dance?
Polka, salsa, fox trot, cha-cha.
Bharatnatyam. Natraj.
Ballet; chassez, plie, arabesque.
Isadora Duncan, Martha Graham, Alvin Ailey.
Revelations.

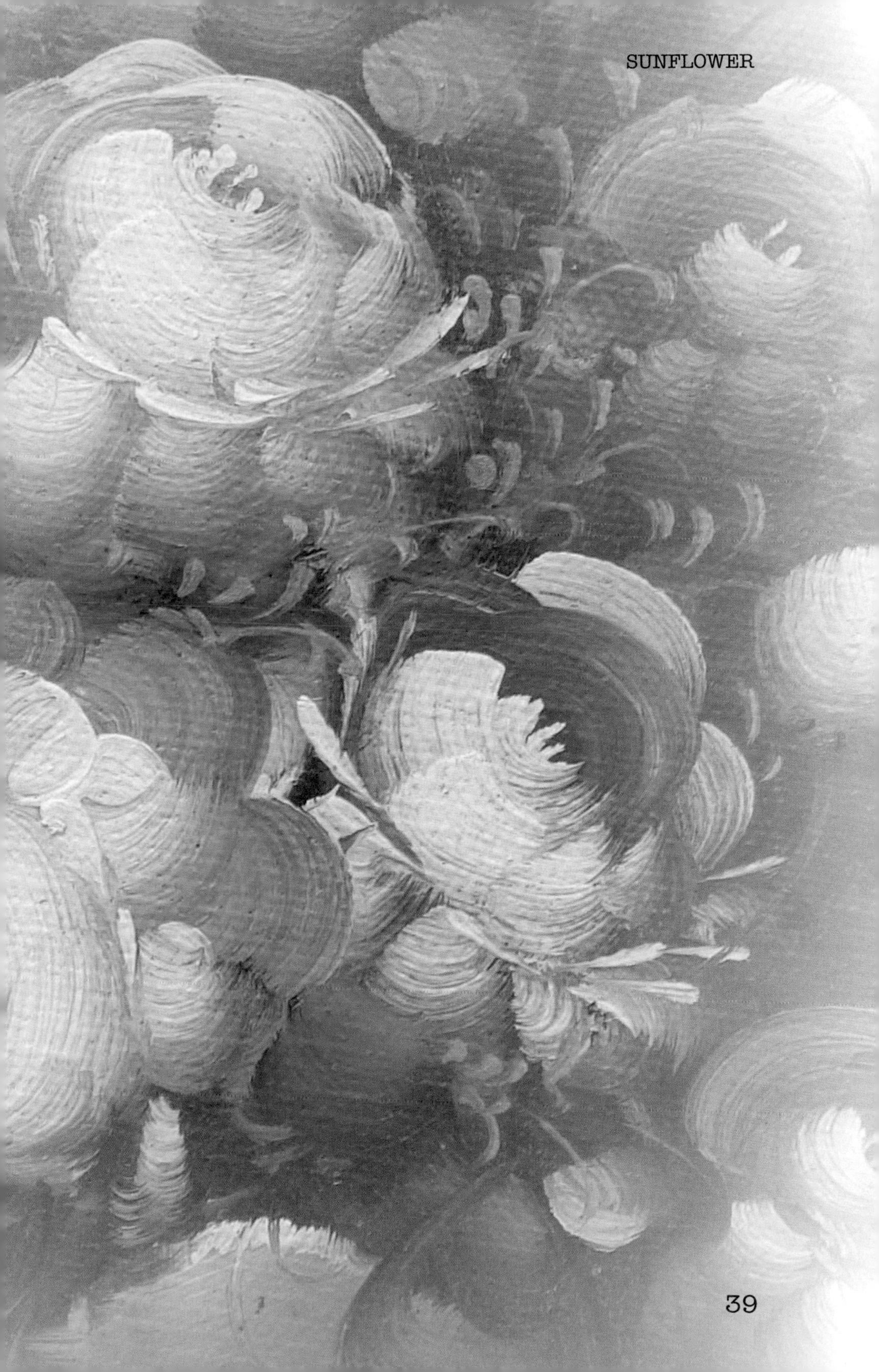

Swan Lake.
Tchaikovsky's Nutcracker.
The snows of an ancient land
 immersed in magic.
The wonderland of beauty.
Poetry. Dance. Blue, white, gold.
Reminiscing. Remembering.
Concentrating. Meditating.
Dancing.

Seasons Winter

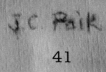

J.C Paik

Walking Alone

60 Korean girls in colorful han-bok,
Scalloped sleeves; red, yellow,
    blue, white, black, green.
Holding hands, encircling the moon.
Spinning. Swirling diaphanous glow.
Cosmic reality. Orbit.
Running clockwise.
And, then, reverse.
Again.
And, again.
The sharp, clear rays of the full moon.
Piercing; receiving. Fullness.
Expectation.
Miracle.
Glory to the Heavens.
Praise to the Father.

The small children were anyway naked.
The tribal females encircled the fire.
Feathers and flowers adorned their hair.
Strings of bone and shell, a ruby or two,
    even a pearl.
Bodies and faces marked and scarred.
Grass skirts.
Top-nude.
Young and old.
Breasts of all shapes and sizes;
Nuts, melons, jugs, sagging and elongated.
Dancing. Gyrating heavy hips.
The men on their drums, in similar fashion.
Orgy of provocation.
By early morning, before sunrise,
    a three year old girl disappeared.

Mountain Home

The scene had vanished.
It was all a dream.
Pure illusion.
Ascendency and descendency.
The dance must continue.
Primordial heart.
Primordial me.
Being. One. Anew.
Don't try defeat.
Avoid misery.
Just. Let. Go.

Verse 3

The man has vanished.
Men in crime. Man
desperate to be relevant.
Women in hard-
core prostitution.
Bullet torpedo tits.
Rocket ass.
Brightly painted face.
More clown than girl.

Esther stood before
me in a dream.
She was dressed in black.
Bright red lipstick
smeared her lips and face.
'Don't you see, Joanie?
It's all a joke.
It's only a joke.'
Then she disappeared
into the dark abyss.

O my hamlet.
Forgive me.
Forgive your
sinful mother.

Sad Clown

Fornicating.
Bastardizing. Spoiling.
To ruin my life is simply
    To obey gravity.
    Time. Law.

A troop of colobus
on the trees;
Bouncing and jumping.
Young and old.
Large and small.
Black and white.
Even Harry.
Harry and I watching.
Together.

Happy Clown

    My good and very hairy dog.
    Here. Praising god.

    Sing hallejujah!
    Shout amen!

47

'Mrs. Sikand, do you want to rock me?'
Yes; of course.
The intellect is a powerful orgasm.
Appreciate, respect, the energy and
 Velocity of your sexuality.
Control. Define. Protect.
Beauty can arise.
Great poetry.
Aware; yet, unaware.
Master of my senses.
Overwhelm me.

Grace. Love.

Royally fucking up your kid.

Creating bastards and misery, sorrow and loss.
Occurrence place and being.
'Hey, that cost money!'
Vincent Ogalo.
Evidence of my life surround me.
What and who I am.
Where I want to go.
Experience and time.
I can find myself anywhere.
'You always make me happy.
You make me smile.'
'Look how smart these ants!
How do they know what to do?'
'When you see this bug—
What you gonna do?'

'Don't kill the ants.'
Humanity descending.
Eroding love and compassion.
Continuing divorce, rupture, loss, sorrow.
A thought thrown out; taking its course.
Emotions. Reactions. Attitudes.
Mindlessness.

You are not feeling anything,
Because you can't.
Inhibitions. Constraints.
Fear of death preventing your escape.

My mother pointed outside the window.
'See the leaves under the bush?
In spring, new grass grow, it's bothering.'
Car accident outside on the corner.
'Anybody hurts?'

My son, twenty-two, upstairs in my bedroom,
Studying.

Maybe Harvard.
God's miracle, yet, again.
The pain of time, that he will leave me
And be a man. To fall in love, to have sex,
To become involved, to feel loss, anger, grief,
Sorrow, yet, again.
Watching helplessly his time to go.

His fear of me his mother. His fear of his dreams and
Subconscious. Compelling him forward.

Eating nuts, berries, seeds, yogurt.
Milky Nescafe.
We have passed her 90th birthday in good celebration.
I am in love.
I am free.

At home.
In the basement.
Returning.
In a dream of happiness and wholeness.

Leaving Chandarana Supermarket.
A tuk-tuk parked and waiting.
John 3:16.
"For God so loved the world."
Brother, we are all servants of god.
The man looked satisfied; ready to go on.

True love, he agreed to octopus.
We sat down and I ordered.
A pretty, silky black lady with a withered white man.
A brown little boy.
Bored.

She was wearing a wig.
The man was on his cell.
When they got up to leave,
His mother lifted the heavy child,
Pulling at her strapless dress.
The boy's left shoe was left under the table.

He truly loved me.
He let me go.
He knew it wouldn't work.
He was too lazy and cowardly to try.
He understood his limits.
So, I couldn't forget.

The crescent moon,
Tethered to its star,
Shimmering through the palm trees.

Black night.

And, the church filled.
The congregation believed,
Faith renewed.
The soul of man still survived.
He arose from the grave.
He remained alive.

Words appropriate to my age and time.
'You are truly full of fuckingshit!'
She meant every word of it.
Everywhere duplicity and lies.
Everywhere greed and lust.
Sorrow.

Captured and imprisoned by ego and desire.
Bound and gagged.
Toss the lovely virgin into
The storming and brewing volcanoe.
Sacrifice to the gods.
Sacrifice your heart and mind.
Do away with yourself urgently.
Hastily.
Laugh and cry.
Scream and cry.
Stay silent.
Briefly consider.
A warning of witches and vipers.
Evil doers.
Wicked sinful ways.
Opening my hands.

My palms and fingers, lines, flesh and skin.
Telling me of my life.
How I was.
Where I am.
Here and now.
Time and space.

(Is Mommy smoking pot right now?
Probably. Let it go. She's Mommy.)
The lines on her flabby stomach
Told of her two children in the womb.
Yes. Indeed she was loved.
Because, she gave love.
She knew love.
From her own wonderful,
Beautiful Mother.

Love was in her every being.
Ancestral pulse and nerve.
A remembered energy and thought.
Anyway, because god, in his mighty way,
Said so.
A heavy appetite for abstentious living.
Denial and grace.
Witness paradise.
Carve out secrets for our success.
No longer thinking of myself.
I am free.

Full moon descending.
Making way for a new day.

Praying yet again for my memory
To remind me.
Recollection of my thoughts, experience, past.
A child. A girl.
A hope. A miracle.
What to do?
Anyway, a girl.
The cold, dry, gray air.
North Korean roots.

Things of pale green, and blue,
Brown, purple, and black.
Things of cold.
Of my womb, above and below.
My wonderful mother.
My very dear son.
My courageous daughter.
And, yes, my dear and beloved husband,
Who pays for everything.
The courage to say I am.

My Mother's hand is still warm.
Hallejujah!
She is still alive.
How great!
How wonderful!
My great love is still here.
Very old.

But still here.
What is praise?
What is worship?
Thanksgiving?
Honor and glory?
Attending church with my Mom, again.
Concentrating on God's word.
Again.
Again in His church.
Again to see stone, brick, wood, light.
Community and congregation
Choosing obedience, love, humility, patience.
Devotion. Study. Time.
Winning favor.
Gaining.
Blessing.
Crying and weeping.
Failing to breathe.
Experience the power of God.
Washing over me.
Baptism. Cleansing. Free.

A baby is born.
A boy.
Close to his mother.
Boyhood games.

'I never bother the highway.'
Halmoni personified everything.
She saw god everywhere.
All had an energy, thought, being.

Yellow is mind.
Yellow is thought, energy, intellect,
Action, decision.
The sun rising above my bed,
Yielding another day.
I am so truly blessed.
Gratitude. Humility.
The quality of being at home.
Yellow roses in a vase of water.
A yellow painting of sunflowers.
The glorious high noon sun casting its yellow glow,
Illuminating.
The world appearing again.
Art dying in a dying world.
Beauty lost and destroyed.
No more great landscapes of simple cottages,
Mountains filtering rivers and lakes.
No more study of the nude with heavy
hair and breasts, shapely buttock.
Only isolation and despair.
No more still life of vases, fruits and flowers.
The pause of a moment, stillness and poetry.
Soft browns, whites, yellows, and greens.
Gone and forgotten.

The Artist

She dressed her best.
No matter her cheeks were
swollen, pussing and red.
She waited for her meeting at
the Four Seasons, ordering
A $20 cappuccino. She
examined the elegant hotel.
She marched into the Korean
Ambassador's office.
Laid out her books.
'My parents raised me Korean!'
Even he was impressed.
He commented on her
impressive lineage.

Current age of immense mediocrity.
Raging stupidity.
Idiots. Morons. Fools.
Destroying themselves.
For the sake of bizarre ignorance.

Yes, she let the Chinese
man in his dumb van
park on the driveway.
Yes, she let the Pakistani
construction man
leave his sign
riveted on the wall
of her house.
'We're all immigrants.
We all need help'
She remembered the
bitter struggle.
She recalled the grace
and providence.
She was ok.

Birds in Flight

SUNFLOWER

65

The crush of the multitudes.
Kapsabet Boys Secondary.
Finally, again at church.
Stop weeping.
Stop crying, NOW!
A bird flew in the assembly.
His nest in the ceiling beams.
Remembering Japanese occupied Korea, 1929.
The pain and suffering.
O Korea.
Bruises, torture, starvation, hunger,
Imprisonment, intimidation.
Occupation. Freezing cold.
Sickness.
My Mother.
'I hate Korea!'
Males. Boys. Pre-men.
Bibles distributed by
The Kenyan Bible Society.

Dancing, singing.
Praising, feeling.
The cry and thunder of 1,000 boys.
"Hallejujah! Amen!"
Strength and youth to believe.

Yet, another day.
Another hope, to continue.
If the sun shines again,
We are again a miracle.
We are again to survive.
Be.
The vast and troubled fruit of
Mother Earth.
A lady pastor spoke.
Quoting the dictionary for the meaning of the word
Trust.
The birds flying in the assembly hall.
Chirping and singing.
The world moved on.
She has healed to face yet
Again another time.
Another day.
The boys hardly wore glasses.
Good skin and teeth.
No pimples or acne.
Good bones.
Smiling. Toughened by work and games.

Good attitudes.
Fresh. Young. Eager. Hopeful.
"Write your stories!
Dream great dreams!
Impossible is always possible!"

Birth and death in the Mara.
Five cheetahs.
A mother with four sub-adult cubs
Feasting on a young wildebeest freshly caught.
Tearing apart the legs and limbs.
Stomach and skull.
Chasing away the jackals and the vultures.
Later, a mother wildebeest gave birth on the open plain.
Danger all around.
The herd keeping watch.
Her placenta dropped.
Later, the young wildebeest calf, fully formed,
Struggling, within minutes, she was following her mother.

Only to live in grace and fear.
The rain clouds passing.
The birds in song.
Pale blue sky.
Pale sun.
Short green grass.
Savannah in light brown.
Soaked by evening rain.
The young on shakey legs,

Somehow knowing where and how to nurse.
Yet dripping of its birth.
Bonding and trusting.
Happiness and joy.

Lightning and thunder against the black sky.
Streaking bolts of light.
Yet, the stars in constellation.

Aquarius, Cancer,
Taurus, Pisces.
The rains started.
Lions grumbled.
Zebras barked.
Bats flew.
An elephant rumbled.
She rumbled all night.
No one could sleep
or get any rest.

By early morning,
Her calf delivered.

　　A boy.

Glad, they joined the herd,
To wander and graze.
Learning of trunks.
Sharpening tusks.
In the sun, moon, stars, and rain.
Mother Earth joyful at her work and play.

Do you get my meaning?

Verse 4

'Thanks for call.
Take it easy.
I lova you.
You are my sunshine.
I miss you all the time.
You're my sweetie pie.
Bye.'

'Mom. President Kim Jong Un
Says he is going to bomb America.'
'He's crazy.
What can you do?'
An age of zombies.
No one thinking.
No one alive.

And so, the mother
elephant gave birth.
As Satao was tragically
poisoned and killed.
Evil, sinful, awful poachers.
The earth however yielding,
fruitfully, generously,
With great forgiveness and love.

Waiting for life to again renew.
Desist. Refrain.
From death, decay, destruction,
Ignorance, stupidity;
Leaving intelligence, goodness,
Morality, strength.

Being buffered by the extremes,
The choices were late.
Strike!
Helping your brother and sister.
The children begging in the streets.
Corruption. Intimidation. Lies.
Manipulation. Fraud. Cheating.
Such poor and slovenly humanity.
Disgrace. Waste. Terrible stinking shit.
The face of immense poverty.
Anger. Guilt. Shame.

Defining myself in the impossible.
Believing I can.
I will.
I AM.

Rhino.
The large, tough, black, male rhino.
The new sun rising, illuminating his flank.
His two horns majestic.
Beautiful. Strong. Curving.
Power lines behind him.
Large rounded shoulders.
Large rounded hips.
His great bronze flank golden, glowing, radiant.
Firm. Taut. Heavy.
His scrotum hanging well. Tight.
He wouldn't mind a female.
He turned and trotted into the remaining
      and badly fragmented savannah
      of what was once greater Nairobi.
The rhythm and horn of the SGR.
The coo of plover.
The shrike call.
White headed fish eagle, perched atop glowing acacia.
The whine and roar of jet engines
 taking off and landing.

SUNFLOWER

Aquaduct

—77—

Some plastic
garbage.
The rising sun,
once cool, now
beating upon
the Earth.
Clouds building
and breaking.

We came upon
acacia shrub
in full flower.
Bees swarming.

Mystical Rabbi gazing at me.
Born of feudal times, I remember.
Pagan rituals adorned,
  I hear song of praise.

Rabbi

Hollow flutes ringing in my ears.
Erect a church within my mind;
  magnificent spirals swirling to
  greater heights.
A young white boy captured by pygmy natives,
  desperate to escape.
Witness paradise.

Religion dying and solar eclipse.
Cancer Moon rising over Eastern Sun.

A fever for your love.
Burning to reunite.
Restless and tired to be apart.
Thinking of you.
Glad you are near.

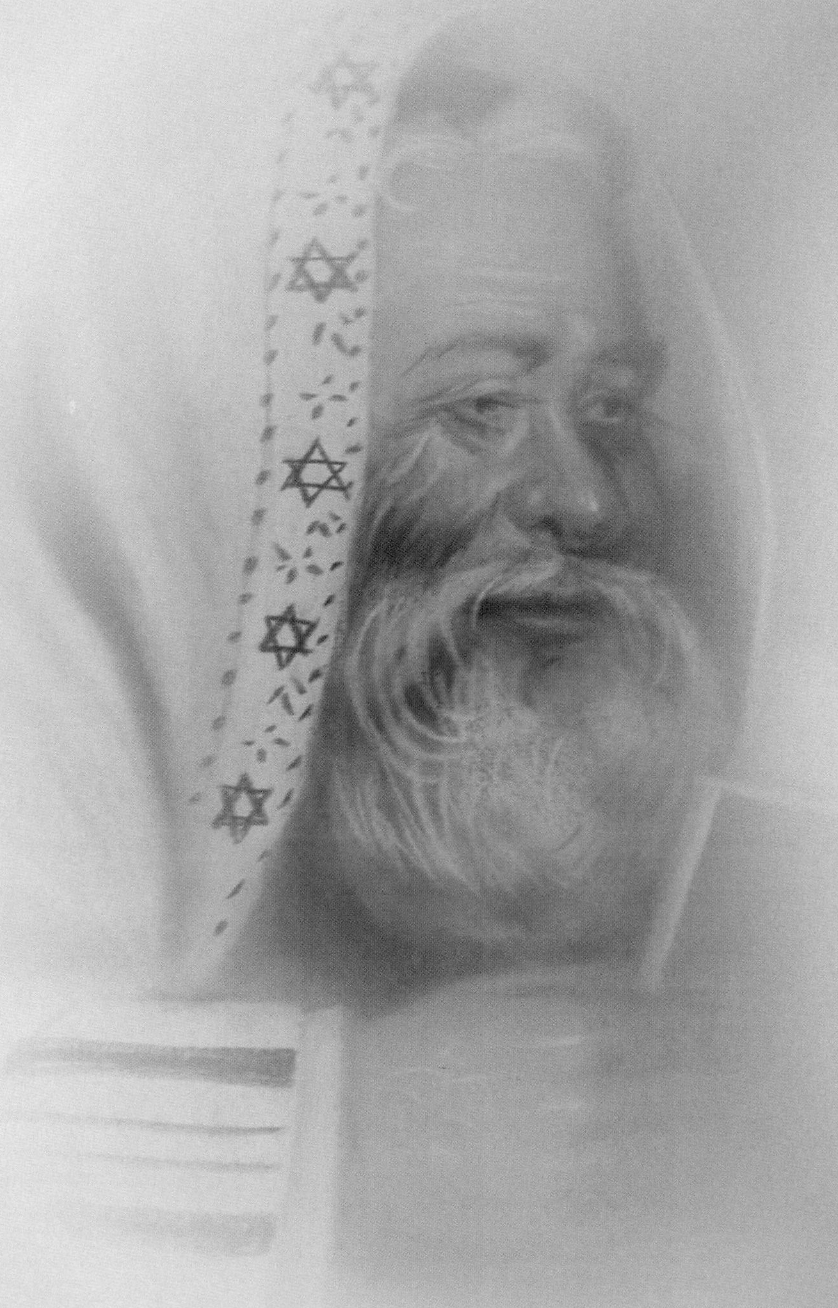

Ghosts and demons cannot harm us.
Unafraid, we are in love.
Together we are blessed.
Truth will always vanquish evil.
Always.
Faith-tested, sure.
Finding infinity in you.

The predictability of our age.
You will eat endless KFC.
You will vote for an idiot.
You will shop and throw it out.
You will fall in fatal love and divorce.
Marketing.
Economy to unravel us.
Break us down.
I feel therefore I am.
The mighty rhythm of god.
Vibrating and coursing through me.
I really don't want anymore – anything.
Not money, wealth, things.
No.
I want you alone, my best friend,
My wonderful companion
To which I am truly and surely your
Everlasting, faithful, good and stable –
Wife.
Believe it so.
Why not?
We are still alive and our
Minds yet alert.

Here and now.
If in no more quality than myself remains,
The joy is mine.
Yes, I can fall in love a thousand times,
But, only once with you.
Oh yes, the very eyes of god upon me.
My husband can see – his very brave wife.
The taming of the shrew.
My hand to serve you.
May it do you ease.

This is the first lesson;
protect and defend your bible.
What word is true?
Keep that one.
Which way to go?
Go there.
Wisdom. Philosophy. Religion. Thought.
Intellect. Belief.

Mountain Home

After 40 years, the sum total of
his ministry was strange.
The pastor's faith had never been stronger;
his convictions only too true.
But, then, why his empty, broken, forgotten
church?
How had the world become so mute, deaf, dumb?
Heart broken, he did not quit.
The doors opened again for
prayer, worship. singing.
And when he won a battle or two,
he could move on.

His faith, at last, was
 perfectly unshakable.
He was on the right path.
He knew it.
God knew it.
This was enough.
More than enough.

We can neither live nor die.
Life a prison
Suicide. Death.
Imprisoned in a lie of immorality,
Lust, sin.
Causing our own miserable destruction

Sunday at the Garden

Out of self-deceit.
Forgetting the truth entirely
 To suit our undiscriminating needs.
Lost.
The decapitated head of St. George.
Failing dragon.
Cut loose a drowning man.
No more men and women.
Only males and females.
Dysfunctional genital differentiation.
Amorphous, dull, stupid.
Raging menopausal depression.
Terrifying realities of fear, hatred, loathing, contempt.
Singular, androgenous, sexless society.
Economic depravity.
Obsessions of the self.

We cannot escape, heal, restore.
Morality and good elude us,
Escape our attention and grasp.
We fail.
We sink.
We despair.
Drowning in self-annhililation and sorrow.
Actions of perversity, crime, neglect, anger , loss.
Dissolving, dissipating thought.
Confused between right and wrong.

The Wailing Wall

Lady with a Black Cat

Averting disaster, to fall into misery.
Definitions no longer have meaning, stance.
Bound by hallucinations, dementias, dreams.

My peers are dead and gone.
Shall I follow?
The loneliness is fatal.
Voting for Hillary.
You can't let America sink that low.
What choice do we make?
Victims of negativity.
Waiting for a miracle.

The wheel will keep on turning.
By turns, living and dying.
By turns healing and failing.
To indeed love and honor death.
Death.
The god, the object.

She evangelized to strangers,
hoping someone would listen.
Convincing people, randomly,
That they can change the world;
That they themselves are
the power of god.
The Korean pharmacist
at Duane Reade.
The handsome young Greek
man on the subway.
The Tibetan woman on
the plane to Spiti.
The Chinese man on the LIRR.
The bald tattooed barber.
The fifteen year old girl
at summer camp.
The thirty-two year old lady at the
clothes shop with huge boobs.
Sicilian Alfred fixing the
basement lights.
Anyone who would stand still
for more than five minutes.
'God is within!'
Always forgive.
No one is perfect.
Error, mistake is there.
Time must continue without
anger, resentment.
Let go.

Man Perplexed

Fishermen

The heroes of forgiveness;
Jesus, Nelson Mandela,
Mother Theresa. Dr.
Martin Luther King.
It can be done.
Be patient.
Watch. Wait.

"I will make you
fishers of men."

God in nature defining me.
Returning balance.
Reminding me of who I am.
Fantastic, fabulous Earth.
Fertile. Fecund. Giving of life.
Air giving tree.
Light giving sun.
Flower, fruit, seed.
Fresh cool early morning dew
Soaking grass, shrub, forest.
Ancient and Judaic
confidence.
Morality. Goodness.
Authority.
Kindness. Me.

A Woman

Yesterday is passed and gone.
Tomorrow is unknown.
The present is here and now.
Things will come and go with time.
Experience and intelligence.
Make way for thought and mind.
Come. Share in my miracle.
Join me.
Journey together.
Trying again in futile attempt
 To hold back time.
A lustrous age of desire. Sexuality.

Yellow is mind.
Yellow is thought, energy, intellect,
Action, decision.
The sun rising above my bed,
Yielding another day.
I am so truly blessed.
Gratitude. Humility.
The quality of being at home.
Yellow roses in a vase of water.
A yellow painting of sunflowers.

The glorious high noon sun
casting its yellow glow,
Illuminating.
The world appearing again.

Very cute baby in a pink top.
No; it's a boy.
Good, sturdy body.
Bright eyes. Two front teeth.
Smiles. Chubby legs,
plump feet, hands, face.
I get to hold the baby
and give him kisses.
The youngest of seven.
Sitting on a park bench.
Where am I going?
Why?
A Chinese mother playing
with her two year old

On a the park stairs
Under the shade of a tree.
The little girl climbing up;
Then climbing down.
Timeless, because of no time.
Pure love. Mother and child.
The good stuff. Old style.
Unconditional.
Yes, we can go on.
Yes, the wheel can turn, yet again.
Pink. Cute.
The baby reached up her arms.
The mother easily took her up and
Held her with so much
joy and delight.
Love.
Very happy. Very sweet.
So many beautiful children.
Each one special.
Where to put them all?
House? School? Food? Health?
Job? Land?
Humanity continuing
into self-annhilation.
How many more roads?

Malls? Restaurants?
Shoe stores? Garbage?
Medicate your children before
sending them to school.
Insure that they must behave
and study at any cost.
Get good grades.
The silence of knowing that
you have messed-up.
Get to work. Make a buck.
Psycho mom.
Wanting one thing after another.
Never enough; never right.
Always angry and upset.
Confused. Confusing her family.
Continuous misery,
jealousy, resentment.
Divorce her sword and weapon.
Massive feminist cover-up.
Lies. Deceit. Fraud. Witchery.
Bitchery. Whore. Black.
"Where did you get that bruise?"
"I can open the garage and
get a baseball bat.
Smash my head in."
"You'd love that, a police report."

Hatred.
In a moment they stopped their
Awful, vicious fight.
Bruised and bleeding,
The husband and wife were
Granted a great and wonderful
Miracle.
Forgiveness.
Indeed, all men were crushed
By her beauty, especially the intelligent,
Masculine, handsome,
tall bearded ones.
Men could recognize her fully and
Failed to breathe; failed to recollect.
My god, she's married.
Worse, she cared way too much.
Getting far too close.
Retreat. Go back. Stay safe.
Forgive.
Be smart. Don't quit.
Yes. Apologise.
'I'm sorry.'

Contrite heart.
Humility. I am no greater than you.
Jealousy is there. Who can judge?
All are human in this wretched age.
Falling. Returning. Remembering love.
Remembering god; in ourselves,
In the scriptures to remind us.
God in our families to bring us
Time and happiness.
God in our world of peace,
Brotherhood, understanding,
Thought, enlightenment.
Awareness and unity with Him, our Father,
Eternal, everlasting, without beginning nor end.
Clear and forever.
Mid-morning sky; blue fading into pale white.
Mountain, thorn trees.
Darker at the canopy.
Dry brittle grass.
Black cotton soil.
Sun rising to bake the earth.

A Broken House

Fruit with Vase

Verse 5

The mother finally understood.
There was no point in praying
For her daughter's marriage.
Such was impossible.
Rather, her prayers turned then to the personal;
How to avoid suffering? Loneliness?
Regret? Loss?
She herself pined for her 90 year old mother.
Japanese occupation.
Communist war.
Imprisonment.
Leaving her mother and Korea forever.
Four daughters; two disabled.
Countless beatings and abuse.
The church.
Raising the church from nothing.
So many deaths. So much pain.
The body needing to rest, return.
Finish. Make way. Retire.
Silence provided answers.
Quiet showed the way.

Patience, fortitude.
Staying alert; waiting.
Rising and falling; and,
Rising and falling again.
No judgment.
No value.
No attachment.
No clinging.
Letting go.
Let it be.
How can life take shape?
Which way? Where?
Mind ever-changing.
History. Time.
Kings and queens of distant lands.
Wars, armies, swords, guns, battleships, bombs.
Donkeys, carts, cars, planes.
Shrines, temples, cathedrals, churches, mosques.
Populations heaving.
Flood, tornadoes, hurricanes, droughts.
Man's hopeful awakening.
Drum, pipe, guitar, song, symphony, ensemble,

Daisies

Joan

Band, screaming hell,
covered in switchblades,
Skulls and skeletons.
Razor in my hand.
Weeping tears of blood.
Wondering, who I am.
What is my character?
Being? Stature?
How do I think?
Speak? Feel? Act?
How did my physical
person begin?

Grabbing a snack before
boarding the train.
A couple with a baby in
the pram also waiting
at the platform.
Struggling to find something.
Running from country
to country.
Planes, trains, buses, roads.
Going nowhere. Lost.

Verse 6

Looking in the wrong direction.
Failing completely to look within.
No song.
No painting.
No dance.
Art is dying.
Mind is degenerating.
Violence and hatred ascending.
Humanity failing.
Sexuality gone beserk;
 Breeding dogs and rats.
In my life what will I do?
What will I achieve?
As Mother Earth defends herself,
 Destroys and punishes
 Will I survive? Gain? Serve? Respond?

SUNFLOWER

Every raindrop will find the ocean.
The sun will rise and fall.
The moon will glow.
We will continue.
Journey. Time.
My death.
My life.
My all.
The world converging into annihilation.
How many people can we put in jail?
The whole world?
Everyone in crime.
Everyone in wrong, harm, injury.
Insanity an accepted demographic; the new norm.
Derangement gone beserk.
Destroying itself with shear stupidity.

Fornicating endlessly;
On a wheel of pure disaster.
No beauty.
Only lots of computers,
machines, buildings.
Food.
On and on, consuming,
engorging.
Pity the children. Sorrow
for the young.
Tether me o my precious
sacred mother,
To this world.
Tie me to your generous bosom.
I thirst for glory and salvation.
Thanking you for
peace and love.
Longing for your
presence and calm.
A mother guided by
her children.
Responding instinctively,
immediately
To their needs and wants.
Intelligence, wisdom, maturity.
Positive choices and decisions.
Whole-hearted
unconditional love.
Love for her child.

Mountain Stream

One way, no return.
No guilt, manipulation or curse.
'Go ahead,' she whispers,
 'Be free. I love you.'

The people are sick.
Falling ill.
Constant grief and sorrow.
No healing anywhere.
Only decay.
What to do?
Yes, pray.
'O great Holy Father,
Grant me your peace,
Your everlasting joy,
Born of forgiveness,
tolerance, compassion,
Deep fellowship;
True and constant love.'

The Nude

Verse 7

What can you say of Korea,
O my America?
The fighting, cold, hunger,
Killing, ruin?
I see my shadow, and therefore,
I know I must be alive.
The early morning sun falling again
Against myself.
My face in black silhouette.
My physical outlined by a
Break against the sun's rays.
The constant pain tells me,

Yes, yet, I am alive.
Blood in my bones;
My back;
My vagina;
My womb;
My face;
My person;
My self.
I am alive.
My poetry.
Calling yet again to a voice unknown.
Whispering yet again a message,
A writing, a knowledge.
Teach me yet again,
O my master,
O my mind.

I am never alone.
I am not alone.
This journey, someone comes with me.
This way, I have company, a companion.
It's you, with me.
Together. Not alone.
Step by step, we follow.
Bracing ourselves against the fall.
Holding ourselves erect against
Gravity and death.
Defeating time and space.
Duality.
You and me.
Us and them.
Embellished by my thoughts.
Disdaining, deferring, defeating desire.
I am free.
Loving you. Caring for you.

Her daughter couldn't sleep.
Caught in a stress of right and wrong.
Swiftly changing times.
Speeding events.
Whiplash humanity.
Morphing and morphing.
Sleep was allusive.

Too much to do.
No time for rest.

Waking up by the Indian Ocean
 Pre-dawn.
Calm. Silent.
Swimming in the low tide.
Sun rising.
Jagged coral.
In the cool, shallow water,
Small fish darting in and out of the porous corals.
Seaweed, sea-grass.
A school of tiny silver-fish
Yellow turquoise striped fish.
Black fish.
Sun rising, heating the earth.
High noon.
Time, changing yet again.
Voices, persons, doing, moving, speaking,

Reacting.
Being.
In the hot sun.
Trees in jubilant splendor.
Towering date palm.
Sprawling neem,
Its roots snarling and extending
Like a giant python.
Frangipani, bougainvilla, cicada.
Trees glorifying the sky and earth,
Reaching and calling heaven.
Soaking and taking in the fierce sun;

Stretching towards the sky,
Leaves, branches, trunk.
Embracing.
The changing tides.
Coming and going.
Every sun and moon, changing.
Sea rising, gently, slowly, in time.
Peace and harmony.
The sun yet rising again.

Raging Sea

The sun yet offering us, kindly,
For another chance to change.
A miracle .

An age of insatiable markets.
Total waste.
Feministic rage.
She understood, finally,
That everything is as it should be, and,
She forgave herself for everything.
She let go.
God is always in control, without fail.
Never-ending truth.
Eternal. Real.
Free.
The seasons will change.

Swallows, ducks, geese in flight.
Rising anew.
I am home again.
Safe. Warm.
Security surrounds me.
My Mom.
I am at peace.
I have returned, once again.
Such peace and rest overwhelm me.
Pain free.

Family

Familiar things surround me;
Offering their memories.
At home, ok.

This world swirling and spiraling into chaos.
Anger. Hatreds.
War, yet again.
Syria, South Sudan, Nigeria, Palestine.
Everywhere, constant struggle.
Always conflict.

128

Notes

Notes